NYC TRAVEL GUIDE

HUNGRY
PASSPORT

How to use this guide?

SECTIONS ARE DIVIDED BY COLORS

SECTION I

Things to know before you go

Packed with practical info from how to get from the airport to Manhattan, how to get around the city, the best time to visit, the best apps to use, which tours to take, etc.

SECTION II & III

Top 10 attractions & 10 additional ones

The absolute must-see 10 attractions, especially if you are visiting for the first time. If you have more time, find additional impressive NYC landmarks and experiences.

SECTION IV

Itineraries, Day trips, Things to do when...

If you don't have the time to plan your own itinerary, you'll find things to do if it's raining, in the winter, in the evening, best day trips, and more.

THIS GUIDE IS INTERACTIVE

Scan the QR code

- **Maps**
- **Tickets**
- **Apps**
- **Info**

TABLE OF CONTENTS

Section 1

Things to Know Before You Go | 5

Section 2

Top 10 Things to Do | 25

Section 3

10 Additional Things to Do | 59

Section 4

Itineraries, Day Trips, etc. | 81

Main MAP

Includes top 10, additional 10 attractions & more

Section 1

Things to Know Before You Go to NYC

This section includes:

I.	General Info	6
II.	Money	8
III.	Weather & Climate	9
IV.	Transportation	10
V.	Food & Drinks	16
VI.	Accommodation	17
VII.	Good to Know	18
VIII.	Apps	20
IX.	City Passes, Tours, Best Views	21
X.	Brief History of NYC	23

GENERAL INFO

Facts & Info About NYC

Population: 8.82 million (2021)
Land area: 303 mi² (784 km²) over 5 boroughs: Manhattan, Brooklyn, Queens, Bronx, and Staten Island
Best time to visit: April-June, September, October
For how long: Min. 5 days
Currency: U.S. Dollar - USD ($, US$)

Covid-19 updates

Official tourist info

US Visa info

NYC events

Drinking Water

It is totally safe to drink tap water in NYC. There are many free drinking water fountains throughout NYC.

Toilets

While there are public restrooms in NYC, finding one close to you may be a little challenging. However, you can use the toilets at the museums, malls, cafés, etc.

Safety

Crime info

New York is one of the safest big cities in the U.S., with an overall crime rate lower than the national average. Beware of pickpockets. Watch your valuables, and use common sense.

Emergency services number: 911

◄ **NYC Crime rate map** (areas to avoid)

Type A

Type B

Power Plugs

Power plugs used in the United States are **type A** and **type B**.

Travel Adapters

If you are coming from outside US, you will need a travel adapter to charge your phone & other devices.

Wheelchair access

Accessibility

The majority of NYC's most popular attractions are wheelchair-friendly. Note: the subway system is crowded and only partially accessible.

◄ **Wheelchair accessible travel guide**

MONEY

Currency

$ - U.S. Dollar is the official currency of the USA and its territories.

$1 is worth approximately:*

€ 0.87 EUR
$ 1.27 CAD
$ 1.39 AUD
£ 0.74 GBP

¥ 116 JPY
₽ 75 RUB
₹ 75 INR
$ 20 MXP

Current rates

Data for Jan. 2022

Credit Cards

Most hotels, stores, and restaurants in NYC accept major credit cards like Visa or Mastercard.

TIP: it is wise always to have some Dollars in your wallet.

ATMs

There are plenty of ATMs in NYC, use Google Maps or a similar app to find one.

WEATHER & CLIMATE

NYC has a humid **subtropical climate**.

Spring

68 °F
20 °C
Average High

In Spring, the weather is **unpredictable**. Rain and even snow is common.

36 °F - 81 °F
2 °C - 27 °C

Summer

82 °F
28 °C
Average High

Hot and humid. Most days are sunny with **thunderstorms.**

61 °F - 84 °F
16 °C - 29 °C

Fall

61 °F
16 °C
Average High

In the Fall, the weather is **mild**, and usually stable, with some rain.

32 °F - 77 °F
0 °C - 25 °C

Winter

45 °F
7 °C
Average High

Cold and damp. Snow is most likely to fall in Jan. and Feb.

27 °F - 52 °F
−3 °C - 11 °C

TRANSPORTATION

From and to John F. Kennedy International Airport in Queens

John F. Kennedy International Airport in Queens is located approx. **16 miles** (26 km) from Manhattan. You can use any of the following means of transportation:

AirTrain: to go to subway

City bus - Via Routes Q3, Q6, Q7, Q10, Q10 LTD, B15

Shuttle | Shared rides ▾

Go Airlink

Air Shuttle

Taxis

A flat fare to get to Manhattan: 52-56^{50} USD

Uber & Lyft

Car rentals

Private car, van transfers

AirTrain: Fast & free way to move around JFK, connecting terminals to parking lots, shuttles, car rentals & NYC public transportation, including the subway.

NOTE: *To get to Jamaica & Howard Beach stations it costs 7^{75} USD, payable only by Metrocard (Subway fares are separate).*

JFK website

Public transport. options

From & to LaGuardia Airport (LGA) in Queens

LaGuardia Airport (LGA) in Queens is located approximately **8 miles** (14 km) from Manhattan. You can use any of the following means of transportation:

City bus - Via Routes M60 & Q70

NYC MTA buses also provide connections to subway, Long Island Rail Road, and Metro-North Railroad

Shuttle rides ▾

Go Airlink NYC

SuperShuttle

Taxis

Uber & Lyft

Car rentals

Private car, van transfers

LGA website

Public transport. options

From & to Newark Airport (EWR) in New Jersey

Newark Liberty Int. Airport (EWR) in New Jersey is located approx. **17 miles** (27 km) from Manhattan. You can use any of the following means of transportation:

AirTrain

> AirTrain connects EWR with Airport Station, where you can take a NJ Transit or Amtrak train to New York's Penn Station in Midtown Manhattan.

Shuttle buses ▼

Coach USA

Go Airlink NYC

SuperShuttle

Taxis

Uber & Lyft

Car rentals

Transfers

EWR website

Public transport. options

Arriving by TRAIN

The two major train stations in New York City are Grand Central Terminal and Penn Station. **Grand Central** is in Midtown on the East Side, while **Penn Station** is just below Midtown on the West Side.

Many train lines are operated by **Amtrak**, **AirTrain**, and **Long Island Rail Road (LIRR)**, as well as intercity bus lines, serve the station.

Amtrak

AirTrain

LIRR

Book train tickets

Arriving by CAR

You can use Google Maps to get driving directions to NYC. You'll also want to know where to park in advance. An app like SpotHero will help you find and reserve parking locations in the city. Alternatively, you can book one of the many hotels in NYC that offer parking.

ParkWhiz

SpotHero

SUGGESTION: Unless you are traveling outside NYC we do not recommend renting or using a car.

Download parking apps

Getting AROUND THE CITY

NYC is well-covered with public transportation. However, you'll still have to walk a lot, so bring comfortable shoes.

Public transportation ▸ MTA: Bus | Subway | Rail

PRICES for bus & subway:
One way: $2^{75} | 1-week ticket: $33
PRICES for railroads (LIRR & Metro-North):
Fares vary based on when & where you are traveling.
You can buy **MetroCard** at the stations (at the vending machines or at ticket desks if available). Or buy a ticket with your mobile phone ▸ **MTA eTix App** (scan the QR code).

Subway MAP

Taxi/Uber/Lyft

Hop-on-hop-off bus

!! Hop-on-hop-off buses are also a part of NYC city passes

Buy tickets with phone

Liberty & Ellis Island ferry

Bikes

Boat rides

Link to trans. options

Hop-on-hop-off ferry

Water taxi

FOOD & DRINKS

We suggest using **Yelp** or **TripAdvisor** to find nearby places with good reviews. Try to avoid restaurants at or next to major tourist sites such as Times Square.

AVERAGE PRICES - bars, restaurants

DRINKS
Coffee	$ 1.5-2.5*
Water	$ 1.5-3
Soda	$ 2-3
Beer	$ 5-8
Wine	$ 6-11
Cocktail	$ 10-20

FOOD
Pizza slice	$ 1-5
Bagel	$ 2-6
Hotdog	$ 2-3
Sandwich	$ 4-8
Lunch**	$ 10-20+
Dinner**	$ 20-30+

*   Coffee at Starbucks or similar: around $5
** Cheap eats: up to $10 | Mid-range: up to $30 | Expensive: from $30

Cheap Eats, Unique Bars and Restaurants

- Los Tacos No. 1 (Chelsea Market)
- Ess-a-Bagel
- The Dead Rabbit NYC
- Trailer Park Lounge
- Beetle House
- Oscar Wilde, etc.

See map for more ▶

Unique Spots

ACCOMMODATION

Attractions in NYC are spread out, especially in Manhattan, so basically anywhere you stay. You will probably be close to at least one attraction.

Average hotel price per night:

from **$200**

TIP 1: The price varies depending on the location, facilities (level of luxury), weekdays vs. weekends, and seasonality. Also, pay attention to extra charges like parking, taxes, etc.

TIP 2: You can find better deals if you take the time to research multiple online booking platforms like Airbnb or Booking. Be flexible with the dates and book accommodation with cancellation options.

To stay close to major attractions:

Midtown, Lower East Side, East Village, Upper West Side

If you want to save some money:

Stay in other boroughs, e.g., Queens

You should know:

(1) **New Jersey:** it is not served by NYC public transport. If you choose to stay there, you will have to commute to Manhattan.

(2) **Apartment rentals:** according to state law, it is illegal in most buildings (there are some exceptions) to rent apartments in NYC for less than 30 days.

GOOD TO KNOW

Tipping

You should always tip at restaurants, bars, and hotels as well as taxi drivers in the United States.

The normal rates are:

- **Wait staff at restaurants:**
  between 15% and 20% pre-tax

- **Bartenders:**
  $1 to $2 per drink
  OR 15% to 20% of the bar tab

Lines & Crowds

With over 8 million people in a relatively small space, NYC is a very crowded place.

Be prepared to wait in line or buy a **skip-the-line ticket** or city pass where you can save on attractions and enjoy skip-the-line privileges.

▸ **See City Passes (page 21) for more information**

Stay connected

Free Wi-Fi

You may be surprised at just how easily you can find many locations with free WiFi – for example, subway stations, parks, coffee shops, museums, tour buses, WiFi kiosks, etc.

Internet

You can purchase a **prepaid SIM card** to access the Internet on your phone.

Alternatively, you can consider renting a **pocket WiFi** or **mobile hotspot**.

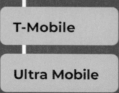

T-Mobile

Ultra Mobile

Pocket WiFi

Links

APPS

Getting around the city

Google/Apple Maps

Moovit Transport.

Subway MTA Map

Citi Bike Rent bikes

Lime El. scooter

Uber | Lyft

Water & toilets

WeTap | Flush

Download these apps

Restaurants, reviews, make reservations

TripAdvisor Review, book

Yelp Review, find a table

Open Table Book a table

UberEats | GrubHub

Do things with locals

Eatwith Eat with locals

Airbnb Experiences, stay

Other apps

Eventbrite Party, events

Viator Book a tour

TodayTix Broadway, etc.

Wifi Finder Find WiFi

City Passes, Tours, Views

The New York City Passes

A great option to save money if you are planning to visit several attractions, skip the line privileges, etc.

CityPASS

New York Pass

GoCity

Sightseeing Pass

NYC passes

Best City Views

Best free views
- Staten Island Ferry
- Brooklyn Bridge
- Pebble Beach

Best paid views
- One World Observatory
- Edge
- Top of the Rock
- Roosevelt Island Tram, etc.

View MAP for more

21

City Tours

Walking tours are organized by professional guides who know a great deal about the city's rich history. Some providers even offer free and pay-what-you-wish tours.

Book your favorite tour

Free OR pay-what-you-wish tours

NYC in One Day Guided Tour

Gangsters and Ghosts Tour in NYC

Graffiti & Street Art Walking Tour

3 Neighborhoods: Soho, Chinatown, Little Italy

Catacombs by Candlelight

NYC Slavery & Underground Railroad Tour

Lower East Side Food and Culture

Brooklyn Half-Day Food and Culture Tour

Craft Cocktails and Speakeasies Tour

Brief History of NYC

With a population of over 8 million people, New York City is one of the largest cities in the world. NYC has a lot to offer: from amazing public parks and green areas, architectural marvels, restaurants with an international flair to an array of museums, colorful art scene, and nightlife.

EARLY HISTORY

NYC was inhabited by Algonquian Native Americans & Lenape, who were hunters, fishermen, and farmers.

16TH CENTURY

Europeans started exploring the region. Italian Giovanni da Verrazzano was the first to discover New York in 1524.

17TH CENTURY

New Amsterdam: Dutch settlement established on today's Governors Island was moved to Manhattan once purchased from the Native Americans. The British seized New Amsterdam from the Dutch in 1664 and gave it a name: New York City. Inhabitants included immigrants from Europe and African slaves.

18TH CENTURY

In 1776 NYC served as a British military base until 1783 when George Washington conquered it. The city started flourishing as a cotton economy and an important port. From 1789 to 1790, NYC was the capital of the US.

19TH CENTURY

Immigrants from Germany, Ireland, and other parts of Europe started their businesses and joined trade unions and political organizations. NYC has grown from around 60,000 to 3.4 million people.

20TH CENTURY

In the early 20th century, African Americans moved to NYC during the Great Migration from the American South. In 1925 NYC became the world's largest city of that era.

In 1965 many people from Asia, Africa, the Caribbean, and Latin America were able to move to the US and revitalize its many neighborhoods.

As a result, NYC we know today is the most diverse city in the world. More than 800 different languages and dialects are spoken on the streets of New York City, and around 37% of the population comes from outside the US.

Because of deindustrialization, many people lost their jobs in the 1970s, and economic problems and criminal activities were on the rise.

21TH CENTURY

WTC complex was rebuilt after the 9/11, 2001, terrorist attacks. NYC is still one of the world's busiest cities and a global business and culture hub.

Top 20
MAPS

Top 10 Things to Do in NYC

This section includes:

1.	Times Square	27
2.	World Trade Center Complex	29
3.	Parks	33
4.	Iconic Buildings	37
5.	Interesting Neighbourhoods	41
6.	Museums	45
7.	Grand Central Terminal	49
8.	Brooklyn Bridge	51
9.	Wall Street	53
10.	Liberty & Ellis Island	55

Times Square

. . .

One of the busiest pedestrian areas in the world

———

1

ENTRANCE FEE

Free

OPENING HOURS

24/7

Location

Times Square, one of the busiest pedestrian areas in the world, attracts over 50 million visitors every year. It is famous for its **enormous electrified ads** creating a surreal neon atmosphere, famous theatres, shopping, and dining.

Times Square got its name from the **New York Times Tower**, headquarters of the New York Times newspaper built in 1904, when the area, which was before known as Longacre Square, became the epicenter of New York's social elite. The first electrified ads appeared in the square also in 1904.

Times Square is also the center of New York's entertainment industry with its **Broadway Theater District** and the venue of **New Year's Eve ball drop**, which is probably one of the most famous New Year's Eve events in the world.

i **Don't miss:** At 11:57 pm, the screens on Times Square transforms into a three-minute art show

2a

Buy ticket here

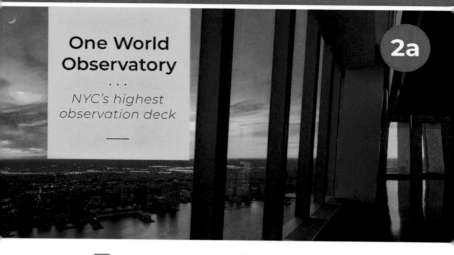

One World Observatory

...

NYC's highest observation deck

—

2a

ENTRANCE FEE
—
From $38

OPENING HOURS
—
10am-7pm
Thursday-Monday

Location

One World Observatory is an observation deck situated on the top floors of One World Trade Center, (Freedom Tower), the tallest building in North America and the tallest building on the Western hemisphere. Set 1776 feet (541 meters) above New York, it offers impressive panoramic views of the city.

You will enter the Observatory through an impressive **elevator ride featuring a virtual time-lapse** recreating the development of New York City's skyline throughout history.

Upon entering the observatory, there is a short video presentation about New York. In the end, the screen rises and reveals the New York skyline below.

i **Did you know?** One World Trade Center is the main building of the area known as the World Trade Center complex, rebuilt after the 9/11 terrorist attacks

9/11 Memorial & Museum

. . .

A place to remember those who died on 9/11

———

Location

OPENING HOURS

———

10am-5pm
Daily, Memorial

10am-5pm
Thu-Mon, Museum

ENTRANCE FEE

———

Free
Memorial

$26
Museum

The **9/11 Memorial** is located where the World Trade Center towers once stood, represented by two square reflecting pools. Don't miss The Survivor Tree, a tree that survived the 9/11 attacks.

9/11 Memorial & Museum honors the victims who were killed on September 11, 2001 attacks and the 1993 World Trade Center bombing.

Don't miss the **Oculus**, an impressive terminal station on the PATH system, part of the World Trade Center complex, which peacefully blends with the surrounding architecture.

i **NOTE:** The 9/11 Museum is also part of the memorial, but you must buy a ticket in advance.

3a

Little Island @Pier55

Parks

. . .

*An escape from
busy streets*

———

3a

Bryant Park

Parks, etc.
MAP

New York City is home to hundreds of parks and recreation areas, offering a great escape from the busy city streets. Don't skip the following ones:

- **Little Island** is an artificial island park on the Hudson River with multiple venues (opened in 2021).

- **Bryant Park** is a small park located outside Main Library, with seating areas. ▶

- **The High Line:** a 1.5-mile (2.3 km) long elevated park, built on a former railroad spur, full of green areas.

- **Battery Park** includes Castle Clinton, a former fort, and other artworks.

- **Washington Square Park & Arch** is a popular place for New Yorkers to meet, relax, and engage in different activities.

- **Prospect Park & more**

Other green areas:

Zoos: Queens Zoo, Bronx Zoo, Central Park Zoo, Prospect Park Zoo

Botanic gardens: New York Botanical Garden, Brooklyn Botanic Garden

---

i **Don't miss:** green areas like zoos & botanic gardens

3b

Central Park
. . .
America's most visited urban park

———

Central Park, **the most visited urban park** in the United States, is probably one of the most famous parks in the world.

It spreads across 778 acres and features lakes, meadows, impressive buildings, and more.

Central Park was approved in 1853, and the first public areas opened in 1858.

Central Park is also a very popular recreation spot.

Don't miss the Upper 5th Avenue that runs alongside Central Park, nicknamed The **Millionaires Row**, home of some of the wealthiest people on earth.

Main attractions ▸

Parks - MAP

- **Sheep Meadow**, a great picnic place
- **Bethesda Terrace** & Fountain
- **Bow Bridge**
- **The Ramble forrest** with Azalea Pond
- **Belvedere Castle**
- **Gapstow Bridge** & The Pond
- **Cleopatra's Needle**, an ancient obelisk
- **Central Park Zoo**
- **Ice skating rinks**, etc.

i **Tip:** rent a boat and experience New York City from a different angle ▸ **The Loeb Boathouse**

3b

The Loeb
Boathouse

4a

SEPHORA

The Vessel tickets

EDGE tickets

Inside the Vessel

Iconic Buildings
. . .
Forming the unique skyline

4a

VESSEL & EDGE

Vessel is a unique 16-stories-high structure with a spiral staircase. Don't skip the **Edge**, the highest outdoor sky deck in the Western Hemisphere also located on Hudson Yards.

FLATIRON BUILDING

Completed in 1902 it is referred to as "one of the world's most iconic skyscrapers." Initially called the Fuller Building, be-cause of its triangular shape & resemblance to a clothes iron.

CHRYSLER BUILDING

Completed in 1930, it was the tallest in the world at the time of its completion. It is consid-ered one of the most influential buildings of Art Deco, known for its seven glowing terraced arches.

Iconic Buildings

. . .

Forming the unique skyline

____

4b

EMPIRE STATE BUILDING

Chrysler Building was the tallest building for only 11 months, when it was surpassed by another Art Deco landmark skyscraper, the Empire State Building, completed in 1931. The building got its name from New York City's nickname – "The Empire State" and features an observation deck.

Observation decks: 86th and 102nd Floor Observatory

30 ROCKEFELLER PLAZA

It was built in 1933 & is best known for its NBC headquarters and observation deck. It is a part of Rockefeller Center, a 19-building center and a plaza created by the Rockefeller family, wildly popular during the Christmas season because of its abundantly decorated Christmas tree.

Observation deck: Top of the Rock

Iconic buildings MAP

4b

Top of the Rock: a view towards
The Empire State Building

Empire State
Build. tickets

Top of the
Rock tickets

Little Italy & Chinatown

· · ·

Manhattan's cultural heritage

———

5a

Little Italy or *Piccola Italia* was once a large settlement of Italian immigrants. It was a known mobster meeting place. In fact, you can even take a mafia walking tour. The movie Godfather also takes place in Little Italy. Today Little Italy is still home to several Italian restaurants and cafés.

The majority of the original Italian population relocated and Little Italy is shrinking with Chinatown on one and upscale **SoHo** full of art galleries and boutiques on the other side. Don't miss charming **NoLita** (North of Little Italy) neighboorhood.

Location

Chinatown is home to the largest ethnic Chinese population in the Western Hemisphere, estimated between 90,000 and 100,000.

The neighborhood is full of Chinese restaurants, shops, as well as other cultural organizations, and, for example, the Museum of Chinese in America.

i **Tip:** Join SoHo, Little Italy & Chinatown guided tour

5b

Interesting neighbor-hoods
. . .
Other impressive neighborhoods
—

MANHATTAN:

TriBeCa (Triangle **Be**low **Ca**nal Street) is home to the Tribeca Film Festival, established after 9/11 to revive this area.

SoHo (South of **Ho**uston Street) features typical cast-iron buildings, home to luxurious shops, pop-up stores, bars, restaurants, etc.

NoHo (North of **Ho**uston Street) is a small but vibrant neighborhood with a diverse culinary, art scene, etc.

Greenwich Village offers bars, cafes, restaurants, Off-Broadway theaters with an LGBT-friendly vibe.

East Village is known for its vivid nightlife, bars, sidewalk cafes, restaurants, boutiques.

Others: Harlem, Chelsea, Hell's Kitchen, etc.

OTHER BOROUGHS:

South Williamsburg, Brooklyn: it contains its original character in its manufacturing past with an art scene, hipster culture, and lively nightlife.

Jackson Heights, Queens: a multicultural neighborhood. Home to Little India with Bollywood music shops, etc. You can experience other ethnic culinary choices, like Latin American, Tibetan, etc.

TriBeC

6a

Tickets for museums

Museums

. . .

NYC as one of the world's leading art hubs

6a

SOLOMON R. GUGGENHEIM MUSEUM

Designed by Frank L. Wright, it is the permanent home to Impressionist, Post-Impressionist, early Modern, contemporary art & several temporary exhibitions.

MoMA

MoMA (Museum of Modern Art) offers a collection of modern and contemporary art.

It is also home to film, design, and art displays and performances.

NY TRANSIT MUSEUM

Located in a former subway station, it offers a glimpse of New York's complex transit system history. It displays a collection of subway trains from the beginning until now.

45

6b

Museums

. . .

NYC as one of the world's leading art hubs

—

METROPOLITAN MUSEUM OF ART

Also known as "The Met," it displays over two million works between its three locations. The main building located on the Museum Mile is also the location of the famous annual Met Gala fundraiser.

AMERICAN MUSEUM OF NATURAL HISTORY

It is one of the world's most prominent natural history museums. Here you can find everything, from dinosaurs to diamonds.

OTHER INTERESTING MUSEUMS:

- MMUSEUMM
- Color Factory
- Museum of the City of New York
- Museum of the Moving Image

Find even more great museums in our MAP:

Museums MAP

6b

The Met

Tickets for museums

7

Grand Central Terminal

· · ·

A world-famous commuter train terminal

7

ENTRANCE FEE

Free

OPENING HOURS

24/7

Location

Grand Central Terminal is a world-famous **commuter train terminal** in Midtown Manhattan. The building also features shops and restaurants spread out through several different levels.

You will probably recognize the Main Concourse with its **iconic clock** in the middle from the movies, as it is a popular meeting place.

It contains impressive **Beaux-Arts architecture,** which incorporates several notable artworks in its central location.

Grand Central Terminal was was completed in 1913 and is one of the ten most visited tourist attractions in the world.

i **Don't miss:** Whispering Gallery located one level below the Main Concourse

8

MAP of NYC
bridges

Brooklyn Bridge

. . .

*An iconic
NYC landmark*

——

8

ENTRANCE FEE

Free

OPENING HOURS

24/7

Location

Brooklyn Bridge is 1596 feet (486 meters) long and 277 feet (84 meters) tall and is one of the main tourist attractions in New York City.

Upon completion in 1883, it **was the longest suspension bridge in the world** and was the world's first steel-wire suspension bridge.

Did you know that there was once a railway line on the bridge? Today the bridge is open only to personal vehicles, pedestrians, and cyclists, and even commercial vehicles are banned from using the bridge.

Join over **10,000 people who cross the bridge** every day on a large pedestrian and bicycle lane. Enjoy amazing views of Lower Manhattan skyscrapers on one and historic Brooklyn on the other side.

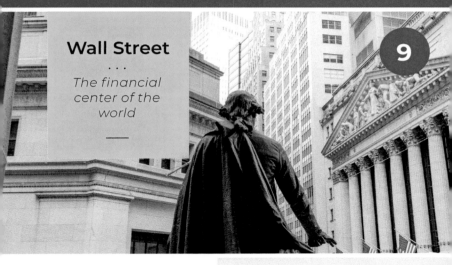

Wall Street

. . .

The financial center of the world

___

9

Location

Wall Street is an actual street located in Manhattan's **financial district**. Over the years, the word Wall Street became a synonym for the American financial markets.

Two of the largest stock exchanges in the world, the **New York Stock Exchange** and **NASDAQ**, are both located on Wall Street.

Most recognizable attractions ▸

- **Charging Bull**, located in the Bowling Green park, is a reminder to keep on fighting, even if the times are bad, for example, during the market crash

- **Fearless Girls:** it sends a message about gender diversity and encourages companies to recruit women to their boards.

- **New York Stock Exchange building**

- **Federal Hall:** a federal-style building & Greek Revival-style building

- **Trinity Church**

- **Mannahatta Park:** New York's Municipal Slave Market, where slaves were auctioned

i **Don't miss:** Charging Bull & Fearless Girl statues

10a

Buy tickets
here

Liberty Island

. . .

Home to the Statue of Liberty

———

10a

ENTRANCE FEE

From $23⁵⁰

Liberty & Ellis Island

OPENING HOURS

9³⁰am-4³⁰pm

Check the website

Location

Liberty Enlightening the World or Statue of Liberty is a 151-feet-tall (46 m) statue located on Liberty Island in the New York Harbor. It **served as a lighthouse** to guide sailors home after a long trip.

The statue was a gift of friendship from the people of France to the United States in 1886. It represents a figure of Libertas, a Roman liberty goddess holding a torch in her right hand and a tablet with the date of the US declaration of independence, July 4, 1776, in her left hand. The statue is recognized as a universal **symbol of freedom and democracy**.

Liberty Island also houses a new Statue of Liberty Museum where the original torch is displayed. It also offers a spectacular view of Manhattan skyscrapers.

i **Did you know?** When the statue arrived in NYC, it was the color of a shiny copper. It took around 20 years for the patina to turn green it is today.

55

10b

Ellis Island

. . .

Entry point for 12 million immigrants

———

Location

OPENING HOURS

9⁴⁵am-3³⁰pm
Check the website

ENTRANCE FEE

From $23⁵⁰
Liberty & Ellis Island

American Immigration Museum on Ellis Island is dedicated to the former immigration inspection station, which operated on the island from 1892 to 1954.

Over **12 million immigrants** arrived in the United States through Ellis Island. The museum offers a glimpse of what it was like for people coming to America for the first time, trying to find a better life. Don't miss Ellis Island **Immigrant Hospital Complex**, which you can only visit with a guided tour.

During the 1812 War, the island served as a fort, and during the Civil War, it was an ammunition supply depot.

‼ TICKETS: buy **one ticket** to visit Liberty and Ellis Island and board in Battery Park, NY, or Liberty State Park, NJ. **Book in advance** as tickets are often sold out.

i **Idea:** Take Immigrant Hospital tour (scan the QR code)

10b

Buy tickets
here

Hospital
complex tour

Top 20
MAPS

10 Additional Things to Do in NYC

This section includes:

11. Chelsea Market	61
12. Comedy Clubs & Stand-ups	63
13. Governors Islands	65
14. Broadway	67
15. Seaport District	69
16. Street Art	71
17. UN Headquarters	73
18. Jazz Clubs	75
19. New York Public Library	77
20. DUMBO	79

11

BIENVENIDOS

Chelsea Market
. . .
*A food &
shopping mall*
—

11

ENTRANCE FEE
—
Free

OPENING HOURS
—
7/8am-10pm/2am
Daily

Location

Located right under the High Line park in Manhattan's Chelsea neighborhood, Chelsea Market is a paradise for foodies, offering **an array of restaurants** from all over the world.

A more proper word to describe Chelsea Market would be "food mall" because of its design when you can walk from one restaurant to the next.

Chelsea Market was transformed into its current form in 1997 from what was originally a factory complex of the National Biscuit Company. Did you know that the **OREO cookie was invented** in this building in 1912? Chelsea Market is owned by Alphabet Inc., Google's parent company.

i **Don't miss:** Los Tacos No. 1, supposedly the best tacos in New York City.

12

Comedy clubs - links

Free stand-up nights

Comedy Clubs & Stand-ups

. . .

Some of the best in the world

12

New York City is one of the world hubs for comedy shows and is home to several notable comedy clubs.

List of some of the best clubs ▸

COMEDY CELLAR

Founded in 1982, big names such as Amy Schumer might drop by

CAROLINE'S

300-seat comedy club, located in Times Square, open all year

NEW YORK COMEDY CLUB

Comedy classics with front bar for pre- and post-show drinks

GOTHAM COMEDY CLUB

Several movies and TV shows were filmed there

FREE STAND-UP NIGHTS:

Free Standup NYC & NYC GO (scan QR codes on the left)

i **Tip:** take advantage of the free stand-up nights. Always check for a surcharge.

13

Gov's Island
Website

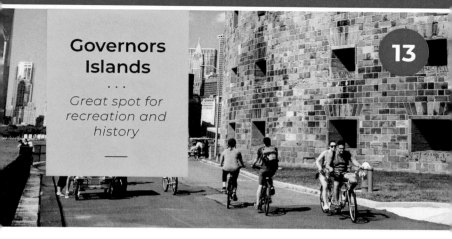

Governors Islands

. . .

Great spot for recreation and history

———

13

ENTRANCE FEE

Free
Ferry ride: $3

OPENING HOURS

7am-6pm
Daily

Location

Governors Island, located in New York Harbor, offers recreation opportunities, especially during the summer. The island is **a former military base** from the Revolutionary War and the War of 1812.

Don't miss many attractions & activities: **(1) Fort Jay**, a star-shaped fort named after John Jay, who was one of the founding fathers of the US, **(2) Castle Williams**, a circular-shaped fort that served for the protection of NYC from the sea, **(3) activities** like biking, kayaking, walking, picnic, camping, watching movies, adventures (zipline, maze, climbing, mini-golf).

The best way to reach Governors Island is by ferry from the Battery Maritime Building in Manhattan and Pier 6 in Brooklyn.

!! Check for modified hours during the winter.

i **Tip:** Ferry is free on Saturdays & Sundays before noon **65**

14

Broadway
tickets

Off-Broad-
way shows

Broadway

. . .

*Musicals for
all ages*

—

14

ENTRANCE FEE

From $30 to $100+

OPENING HOURS

Varies
Check website

Location

Located in Manhattan's Theatre District, Broadway performances are offered in **41 large theaters** with 500 or more seats, attracting over 14 million visitors per year.

The majority of theatre performances on Broadway are musicals. Broadway is considered to offer the highest level of theatre performance in the English-speaking world, and NYC is sometimes referred to as the **cultural capital** of the Western Hemisphere.

While the concentration of theaters and performances is the biggest on Broadway, NYC offers other important **performance centers**, for example Radio City Music Hall, located in the Rockefeller Center, or St Ann's Warehouse at DUMBO.

i **Tip:** visit smaller Broadway shows (off-Broadway
& off-off Broadway shows)

15

Seaport District

. . .

A historical waterfront district

———

Seaport is a **historic waterfront district** with many retail, dining, and cultural options. Located along the East River offers beautiful views towards the Brooklyn Bridge and NYC.

From being the link between the new and the old words in the 17th century, a commercial hub in the 1860s, opening the **Fulton Fish Market** in the 19th century, to being able to adjust to the new ways of development, Seaport played an essential role in trade and commerce.

A new urban development concept was introduced in the 1970s, like the preservation of the old historical buildings like **Schermerhorn Row** with new architectural development. ▶

Location

BEST ATTRACTIONS:

- **Pier 15:** Watermark bar, public pier for picnics
- **Pier 16:** Ambrose & other lightships, outdoor space for concerts, etc.
- **Pier 17:** restaurants (e.g., The Greens, Malibu Farm), rooftop concerts, and other attractions
- **South Street Seaport Museum**
- **New Amsterdam Market:** seasonal marketplace
- **Titanic Memorial Park**
- **Imagination Playground**

16

Flashinvaders
app

Masterpiece
NYC

Street Art

. . .

New York City as an open-air museum

———

16

SPACE INVADERS

Space Invaders are pieces of art made from mosaics glued to the walls and other surfaces by a French urban artist Invader.

The inspiration for the art comes from the **1970s video game** Space Invaders. The art appears overnight in different places all over the world.

You can find them in NYC, L.A., Rome, Hong Kong, and other cities.

People **chase art with their smartphones** using an app called FlashInvaders. You can download the FlashInvaders app (QR

GRAFFITI

While modern graffiti originate in Philadelphia in the 1960s, they have spread to the NYC subway system and beyond. Once guerilla art, it is now an internationally recognized form.

Some of the places where you can find graffiti include World Trade Plaza, The High Line Park, Bowery Graffiti Wall, etc.

i **Tip:** Street art is present in all of the five boroughs. Walk around and explore graffiti and other street art.

17

Reserve UN
tickets here

United Nations
. . .
Headquarters of world's center of diplomacy

—

17

ENTRANCE FEE
—
$22

OPENING HOURS
—
Temporarily closed due to COVID-19

Location

The United Nations Headquarters are located on the east side of Midtown Manhattan. While most people recognize the skyscraper (the Secretariat), the UN Headquarters are a **complex of several buildings**.

General Assemblies, where leaders meet, are held in the building next to the Secretariat – the General Assembly Building.

UN Headquarters are **featured in many movies**, but only two movies, The Glass Wall (1953) and The Interpreter (2005) were filmed inside.

Although the UN Headquarters are located in NYC, the land is considered **international territory**.

!! TICKETS: You can only buy tickets in advance. Guided tours are the only option to see the UN HQ.

i Don't miss: A collection of sculptures (UN garden)

18

Links to NYC
jazz clubs

Jazz Clubs
. . .
Where jazz legends were born

———

18

NYC is the place where the world's most prominent jazz stars perform regularly. In fact, the city has been described as the "jazz mecca." The legends who performed in New York include Miles Davis and Charlie Parker.

Make your stay in New York City unforgettable and visit one of the city's landmark jazz clubs.

As a result, New York City offers an array of jazz clubs and jazz lounges. We gathered the list of some of the most important ones. ▶

IRIDIUM

Live music location that features not only jazz but also rock & blues.

BIRDLAND

One of the best jazz clubs in the world with Cajun-influenced food

BLUE NOTE JAZZ CLUB

Jazz club and restaurant in Greenwich Village

VILLAGE VANGUARD

First focused on folk music, but later became a jazz landmark

JAZZ STANDARD

One of the largest jazz clubs and features new & well-known artists

NUBLU CLASSIC

Live jazz and world music with its own record label

75

19

New York Public Library
· · ·
Landmark Beaux-Art masterpiece
———

19

ENTRANCE FEE
———
Free

OPENING HOURS
———
8/10am-5/9pm
Daily

Location

The Stephen A. Schwarzman Building, dubbed "Main Branch," is the main location of the New York Public Library system. This impressive landmark building is located in Bryant Park in Midtown Manhattan.

It was **opened to the public in 1911** due to a merger of two New York libraries and designed in the Beaux-Art style, featuring numerous impressive rooms. In front of the library, there are statues of two stone lions named Patience and Fortitude. The lion is also a logo of the New York Public Library.

The building was **featured in numerous movies** and TV shows such as Sex and the City, Ghostbusters, and The Day After Tomorrow.

i **Don't miss:** famous staircase where TV series Sex and the City was filmed

20

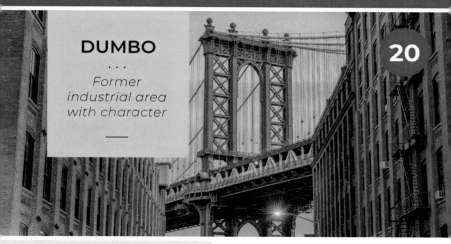

DUMBO

. . .

Former industrial area with character

—

20

DUMBO (**D**own **U**nder the **M**anhattan **B**ridge **O**verpass) is a Brooklyn neighborhood located under the Manhattan Bridge.

The area was a **center of NYC's manufacturing** in the late 19th and early 20th century. It remained relatively untouched even after some significant changes, unlike other similar areas in New York City and other big cities.

Over the years, DUMBO was able to keep its original spirit and is now a popular place for Instagrammers and those who are looking for the **best pizza in town** in one of many popular

Location

restaurants, as well as New York's leading tech hub with numerous well-known technology firms such as Etsy.

Don't miss famous attractions, like the archway, **Pebble Beach**, Empire Stores Warehouse, Brooklyn Flea, St. Ann's Warehouse, Fulton Ferry Park, Main Street Park, Colorful Glass House, etc.

i **Tip:** take a photo of Manhattan Bridge from DUMBO

Section 4

Itineraries, Things to Do, Best Day Trips

This section includes:

1. One Day Itinerary — 82

2. Two Day Itinerary — 83

3. Three Day Itinerary — 84

4. Best Day Trips — 85

5. Things to do... — 87

ITINERARIES

To make your trip to New York City stress-free and organized, we prepared simple one, two, and three-day itineraries. Each suggested itinerary includes a dedicated QR code to a customized Google Map that you can easily use on your phone.

◄ MAP

1-Day Itinerary

Morning

- Brooklyn Bridge
- One World Trade Complex: 9/11 Memorial and Museum, One World Observatory
- Oculus
- Chelsea Market (stop for a quick lunch)
- Little Island - if time

Afternoon

- High Line
- The Vessel
- Bryant Park, Public Library
- Grand Central Terminal
- Central Park

Evening

- Times Square
- Broadway Show

2-Day Itinerary

MAP ▸

Day 1

Morning

- Grand Central Terminal
- Public Library
- Bryant Park
- Times Square

Afternoon

- Rockefeller Center, observation deck
- MoMA or The Met
- Central Park

Evening

- Comedy Club OR
- Broadway Show

Day 2

Morning

- The Vessel
- High Line\
- Little Island - if time
- Chelsea Market
- Washington Square Park (if time)

Afternoon

- Little Italy & Chinatown
- 9/11 Memorial (Museum - if time)
- One World Observatory
- Financial District
- Seaport District (if time)
- Brooklyn Bridge

Evening

- Explore DUMBO
- Jazz Club

◄ MAP

3-Day Itinerary

Day 1

Morning

- Grand Cent. Terminal
- Public Library
- Bryant Park
- Times Square

Afternoon & Evening

- Rockefeller Center, observation deck
- MoMA or The Met
- Central Park
- Comedy Club

Day 2

Morning

- Vessel or Edge
- High Line
- Chelsea Market
- Little Island OR Washington Square Park (if time)

Day 2 - continue

Afternoon & Evening

- Little Italy and Chinatown
- WTC Complex
- Broadway Show

Day 3

Morning

- DUMBO
- Brooklyn Bridge
- Seaport District
- Wall Street

Afternoon

Battery Park to go to: Liberty & Ellis Island

Evening

Jazz Club

Best Day Trips

MAP ▸

Coney Island, Brooklyn

Why visit? A relaxing destination by the water with entertainment areas (e.g., Wonder Wheel, Luna Park).
How far from Manhattan: 20 mi. or 30 km.

Staten Island, NYC

Why visit? More than 170 parks, a botanic garden, a zoo, fantastic nightlife and other attractions.
How far from Manhattan: 22 mi. or 35 km.

Long Island (Fire Island), NY

Why visit? Beautiful sandy beaches, sport activities (surfing, kayaking), whale watching, food and wine.
How far from Manhattan: 55 mi. or 90 km.

Philadelphia, PA

Why visit? Rich history (Liberty Bell, Independence Hall, etc.), delicious food (e.g., famous cheesesteak), activities by the water (Penn's Landing), etc.
How far from Manhattan: 95 mi. or 150 km.

Hudson, NY

Why visit? Unique historical, shopping, dining, lodging, and cultural experience. About 2-hour train ride from NYC.
How far from Manhattan: 120 mi. or 200 km.

All activities
& links

Things to do...

...IN THE SUMMER

- Spend an afternoon at the urban beach, like Newport Sand Beach, New Jersey
- Enjoy outdoor cinemas, like Rooftop Cinema Club
- Visit Governors Island, Coney Island or Brighton Beach
- Take a boat ride
- Attend summer festivals, concerts
- Sports & water activities, like jet skiing, flyboarding, kayaking, etc.
- Visit museums
- Spend an afternoon at a ZOO
- Chill at a rooftop bar
- Visit farmers, food or flea markets

...IN THE WINTER

- Try ice skating at The Rink At Rockefeller Center
- Attend Christmas and other markets, like Bank of America Winter Village
- Visit museums, art galleries, and exhibitions
- Visit winter gardens & indoor plazas, like The Winter Garden, The Ford Foundation Building, etc.
- Go shopping: The Shops at Columbus Circle, Eataly, etc.
- Explore indoor food and other markets, like Chelsea Market

Things to do...

...IF IT'S RAINING

- Attend a cooking/ baking class
- Visit museums, art galleries, and exhibitions
- Indoor skydiving
- Extreme sports, paintball, laser tag
- Escape room
- Roller skating
- Go to the cinema
- Indoor farmers, food and flea markets
- Bowling
- Go shopping
- Explore quirky bars, like House of Wax, Kick Axe Throwing, NO BAR, etc.
- Discover city after the rain, especially Time Square

...IN THE EVENING

- Attend a show, a concert, opera, jazz, stand-up, etc.
- Go to a bar or a nightclub
- Spend a night at the American Museum of Natural History
- Embark on an evening or a night tour
- Observation decks - see the city lights and skyline from above
- Visit some museums opened in the evening, like Brooklyn Museum, etc.
- Enjoy Times Square
- After the rain

All activities
& links

New York City Travel Guide by Hungry Passport
4225 Solano Ave. Ste 63, Napa CA 94558, USA

www.hungrypassport.xyz

© 2022 Hungry Passport Media Inc.

Disclaimer: While we do our best to provide the most current information, opening hours change on a regular basis, businesses close, etc. so we do not guarantee any information in this travel guide is accurate. If you are in doubt, always research on your own. We are not endorsed by any business or other entity presented in this guide.

CREDITS: Cover photo: Adobe Stock | P2: Hungry Passport Travel Guide page mockups, Envato (scanning QR code, mobile phone), Google Maps | P4: Adobe Stock | P6: Twenty20 | P7: 123rf (power plugs & outlet style graphics) | P8 (from above): Envato, Envato, Envato | P9: Envato (Weather Icons) | P10: Twenty20 | P16: Twenty20 | P18: Envato, Envato | P21: Envato | P26: Adobe Stock | P27: Adobe Stock | P28: Pixabay | P29: One World Observatory | P30: Twenty20 | P31: Alex Iby/Unsplash | P32: Adobe Stock | P33: Twenty20 | P34: Envato| P35: Twenty20 | P36: Twenty20 | P37 (from above): Twenty20, James Morehead/Unsplash, Nextvoyage/Pexels, ASSY/Pixabay | P38 (from above): Adobe Stock, 123rf, supergig160/Pixabay | P39: Twenty20 | P40: Adobe Stock | P41: Adobe Stock | P42: Twenty20 (top), Twenty20 (bottom) | P43: Twenty20 | P44: Twenty20 | P45 (from above): KaiPilger/Pixabay, Pipe A./ Unsplash, Twenty20, Hungry Passport | P46 (from above): Twenty20, Twenty20, Twenty20 | P47: Twenty20 | P48: Adobe Stock | P49: Pexels | P50: Envato | P51: Envato | P52: Envato | P53: Twenty20 | P54: Twenty20 | P55: Adobe Stock | P56: Adobe Stock | P57: Adobe Stock | P60: Twenty20 | P61: BreathofO2/Pixabay | P62: Twenty20 | P63: Monica Silvestre/Pexels (top), Envato (bottom) | P64: Twenty20 | P65: Twenty20 | P66: Twenty20 | P67: Twenty20 | P68: Adobe Stock | P69: Adobe Stock | P70: Twenty20 | P71: Twenty20 (top), Hungry Passport (bottom) | P72: Adobe Stock | P73: Adobe Stock | P74: Twenty20 | P75: Chris Bair/Unsplash | P76: Adobe Stock | P77: Adobe Stock | P78: Twenty20 | P79: Envato | P86: Adobe Stock | P87: Adobe Stock (icons) | P88: Adobe Stock (icons) | P89: Adobe Stock | Back cover: Hungry Passport Travel Guide mockup, Envato (scanning QR code) | Icons throughout this guide: Envato & Hungry Passport

Written & designed by Hungry Passport, ©All rights reserved